# Investment ideas in USA

## What to Invest In, Use Your Money to Make Money

Aaron I. Tucker

## Table of contents

# Chapter 1

## HISTORY OF INVESTMENT

The Code of Hammurabi (about 1700 BC) created a legal foundation for investment, creating a way for the promise of collateral by codifying debtor and creditor rights in reference to pledged land. Punishments for violating financial responsibilities were not as harsh as those for crimes involving damage or death.

In the medieval Islamic world, the qirad was a key financial tool. This was an agreement between one or more investors and an agent where the investors committed funds to the agent, who subsequently traded with them in hopes of generating a profit.

Both parties then got a previously determined amount of the profit, although the agent was not accountable for any losses. Many will observe that the qirad is comparable to the institution of the commenda subsequently employed in western Europe, albeit whether the qirad turned into the commenda or the two institutions arose separately cannot be established with confidence.

In the early 1900s, buyers of stocks, bonds, and other assets were labeled by the media, academics, and trade as "speculators." Since the Wall Street crisis of 1929, and notably by the 1950s, the word "investment" had come to designate the more conservative end of the securities spectrum, while the word "speculation" was used by financial brokers and their advertising agencies to refer to higher-risk products that were much in favor at that time. Since the late twentieth century, the terms "speculation" and "speculator" have been explicitly associated with higher-risk activities.

# Chapter 2

## DEFINITION OF INVESTMENT

Investment is the dedication of money to purchase an object to attain an increase in value over a period of time. Investment entails the sacrifice of some present thing, such as time, money, or effort.

In finance, the purpose of investing is to obtain a return from the invested asset. The return may consist of a gain (profit) or a loss realized via the sale of a property or an investment, unrealized capital appreciation (or depreciation), or investment income such as dividends, interest, or rental income, or a combination of capital gain and income. The return may also include currency gains or losses owing to changes in foreign currency exchange rates.

Investors often anticipate bigger profits from riskier assets. When a low-risk investment is undertaken, the return is often modest. Similarly, high risk comes with a probability of significant losses.

Investors, especially beginners, are typically urged to diversify their portfolio. Diversification has the statistical effect of lowering total risk.

# Chapter 3

## INVESTMENT STRATEGIES

### *Value Investing*

A value investor buys assets that they perceive to be cheap and sells overpriced ones (and overvalued ones). To uncover cheap stocks, a value investor employs the study of the financial reports of the issuer to appraise the investment. Value investors apply accounting statistics, such as profits per share and sales growth, to find shares selling at prices below their value.

Warren Buffett and Benjamin Graham are renowned examples of value investors. Graham and Dodd's foundational book, Security Analysis, was prepared in the aftermath of the Wall Street Crash of 1929.

The price-to-earnings ratio (P/E), or earnings multiple, is a very important and recognized fundamental measure, with a function of dividing the share price of the firm by its earnings per share. This will supply the value indicating the amount investors are willing to devote for each dollar of firm profits.

This ratio is an important component because it can be used to compare the values of different businesses.A company with a lower P/E ratio will cost less per share than one with a higher P/E, taking the same degree of financial success into consideration; consequently, it basically suggests a low P/E is the preferable alternative.

An instance in which the price-to-earnings ratio has a smaller impact is when businesses in various sectors are compared. For example, while it is fair for a telecom company to exhibit a P/E in the low teens, in the case of hi-tech stock, a P/E in the 40s range is not uncommon. When doing comparisons, the P/E ratio may provide you with a finer understanding of a specific company's value.

For investors paying for each dollar of a company's profits, the P/E ratio is an important indicator, but the price-to-book ratio (P/B) is also a trustworthy measure of how much investors are ready to spend on each dollar of business assets.
In the calculation of the P/B ratio, the share price of a company is divided by its net assets; any intangibles, such as goodwill, are not taken into consideration.

It is an important aspect of the price-to-book ratio, owing to the fact that it represents the real payment for tangible assets and not the more problematic appraisal of intangibles. Accordingly, the P/B might be regarded as a rather cautious measure.

***Growth Investing***

Growth investors pursue assets they feel are likely to have larger profits or greater value in the future. To find such firms, growth investors generally assess metrics of current stock value as well as expectations of future financial success. Growth investors seek profits via capital appreciation, or the gains realized when a stock is sold at a higher price than what it was acquired for.

The price-to-earnings (P/E) ratio is also employed for this sort of investment; growth companies are likely to have a P/E greater than others in their sector. According to Investopedia contributor Troy Segal and U.S. Department of State Fulbright fintech research awardee Julius Mansa, growth investing is best suited for investors that favor relatively shorter investment horizons, greater risks, and aren't expecting rapid income flow via dividends.

Some investors trace the origin of the growth investing technique to investment banker Thomas Rowe Price Jr., who tested and popularized the concept in 1950 by creating his own mutual fund, the T. Rowe Price Growth Stock Fund. Price argued that investors may reap great profits by "investing in firms that are well-managed in rich fields."

### *Momentum Investing*

Momentum investors often attempt to acquire stocks that are presently enjoying a short-term rise, and they frequently sell them once this momentum begins to subside. Stocks or assets acquired for momentum investing are frequently defined by exhibiting consistently strong returns over the last three to twelve months.

However, in a bear market, momentum investing also entails shorting shares of companies that are undergoing a negative trend, since it is thought that these stocks will continue to drop in value. Essentially, momentum investing often depends on the idea that a regularly up-trending stock will continue to increase, whereas a persistently down-trending company will continue to decline.

Economists and financial specialists have not established an agreement on the usefulness of employing the momentum investing technique. Rather than examining a company's operational performance, momentum investors typically employ trend lines, moving averages, and the

Average Directional Index (ADX) to identify the presence and strength of trends.

# Chapter 4

## TYPES OF INVESTMENT

### What is the most profitable for you?

Investing may terrify a lot of individuals since there are many possibilities, and it can be hard to figure out which assets are suitable for your account. This tutorial leads you through 10 of the most prevalent forms of investment, from stocks to crypto, and explains why you may want to consider incorporating them in your portfolio. If you're serious about investing, it can make sense to locate a financial adviser to assist you and help you figure out which assets will enable you to accomplish your financial objectives.

### 1. Stocks

Stocks, sometimes known as shares or equities, could be the most well-known and straightforward sort of investing. When you purchase stock, you're purchasing an ownership share in a publicly traded corporation. Many of the largest firms in the nation—think General Motors, Apple, and Facebook—are publicly listed, meaning you may purchase shares in them.

How to Make Money: When you buy a stock, you expect the price to rise so that you can sell it for a profit later.The danger, of course, is that the price of the stock may go down, in which case you'd lose money.

## 2. Bonds

When you purchase a bond, you're effectively lending money to a business. Generally, this is a company or a government institution. Companies offer corporate bonds, while local governments issue municipal bonds. The U.S. Treasury issues Treasury bonds, notes, and bills, all of which are debt securities that investors purchase.

How you may earn money: While the money is being loaned, the lender obtains interest payments. After the bond matures: that is, after you've kept it for the contractually stipulated period of time tyou receive your principal back.

Bonds typically have lower rates of return than stocks, but they also have lower risk.There is still some danger involved, of course. The firm you purchase a bond from might collapse, or the government could default. Treasury bonds, notes, and banknotes, however, are regarded as highly secure assets.

### 3. Mutual Funds

A mutual fund is a pool of numerous investors' money that is extensively invested in a number of firms. Mutual funds may be actively managed or passively managed. An actively managed fund has a fund manager who chooses securities in order to place investors' money. Fund managers typically strive to beat a predefined market benchmark by identifying assets that will outperform such an index.

A passively managed fund, commonly known as an index fund, simply follows a major stock market index like the Dow Jones Industrial Average or the S&P 500. Mutual funds may invest in a wide variety of securities, including stocks, bonds, commodities, currencies, and derivatives.

Mutual funds bear many of the same risks as stocks and bonds, depending on what they are invested in. The risk is frequently reduced, however, since the assets are automatically diversified.

How you may earn money: Investors gain money off mutual funds when the value of stocks, bonds, and other packaged assets that the fund invests in goes up. You may acquire them directly via the management company and cheap brokerages. But notice there is normally a minimum commitment, and you'll pay an annual charge.

## 4.Exchange-Traded Funds (ETFs)

Exchange-traded funds (ETFs) are similar to mutual funds in that they are a collection of assets that monitor a market index. Unlike mutual funds, which are acquired via a fund firm, shares in ETFs are bought and sold on the stock market. Their price changes during the trading day, while mutual funds' worth is simply the net asset value of your assets, which is computed at the conclusion of each trading session.

**How you may earn money:**

ETFs are generally advised for beginner investors since they're more diversified than individual equities. You may further limit risk by purchasing an ETF that follows a wide index. And much like mutual funds, you may earn money from an ETF by selling it when it gains value.

## 5. Certificates of Deposit (CDs) (CDs)

A certificate of deposit (CD) is a very low-risk investment. You offer a bank a set amount of money for a certain length of time. When that time period is finished, you receive your principal back plus a fixed amount of interest. The longer the loan term, the greater your interest rate.

How you may earn money: CDs are wonderful long-term investments for saving money. There are no substantial dangers since they are FDIC-insured up to $250,000, which would protect your money even if your bank were to fall. That being the case, you have to be sure you won't need the money during the period of the CD, since there are large penalties for early withdrawals.

## 6. Retirement Plans

There are a variety of types of retirement plans. Workplace retirement plans, provided by your company, include 401(k) plans and 403(b) plans. If you don't have access to a retirement plan, you might get an individual retirement account (IRA), either the regular or Roth kind.

How you can earn money: Retirement plans aren't a different type of investment, per se, but a vehicle to acquire stocks, bonds, and funds in two tax-advantaged ways.
The first allows you to invest pre tax funds (similar to a traditional IRA).The second permits you to withdraw money without paying taxes on that money. The risks of the investments are the same as if you were purchasing the products outside of a retirement plan.

## 7. Options

An option is a considerably more sophisticated technique to acquire a stock. When you purchase an option, you're acquiring the opportunity to buy or sell an asset at a specified price at a certain time. There are two sorts of options: call options, for purchasing assets, and put options, for selling options.

How you may earn money: As an investor, you lock in the price of a stock with the expectation that it will go up in value. However, the danger of an option is that the stock might potentially lose money. So if the stock declines from its starting price, you lose the money from the contract. Options are a complicated investment tool, and individuals should take care before employing them.

## 8. Annuities

Many individuals utilize annuities as part of their retirement savings strategy. When you acquire an annuity, you get insurance coverage and, in exchange, receive monthly payments.

Annuities exist in several kinds. They may endure till death or merely for a certain amount of time. The company may need ongoing premium payments or only one up-front payment. They may relate partly to the stock market, or they may just be an insurance policy with no direct relationship to the markets. Payments may be immediate or postponed for a defined period. They may be fixed or changeable.

How you may earn money: Annuities can ensure an extra source of income during retirement. But although they are quite low risk, they aren't high-growth. So investors prefer to make them an excellent complement to their retirement savings rather than a vital source of financing.

## 9. Cryptocurrencies

Cryptocurrencies are a very new investment opportunity. Bitcoin is the most renowned cryptocurrency, although there are many others, such as Bitcoin and Ethereum. These are digital currencies that don't have any official backing. You may purchase and sell them on cryptocurrency exchanges. Some stores will even let you make purchases using them.

How you may earn money: Cryptos typically have huge volatility, making them an extremely dangerous investment. However, some investors use them as a supplement to stocks and bonds to diversify their portfolios.You may acquire them through bitcoin exchanges.

## 10. Commodities

Commodities are actual items that you may invest in. They are widespread in futures markets when producers and commercial purchaser surin other words, professionals—attempt to hedge their financial position in the commodities.

Retail investors should make sure they properly understand futures before investing in them. Partly, this is due to the risk that the price of a commodity will fluctuate dramatically and abruptly in either direction due to unexpected occurrences.For instance, political acts may dramatically influence the value of something like oil, while weather can affect the value of agricultural goods.

**Here's a breakdown of the four main types of commodities:**

-

- Metals: precious metals (gold and silver) and industrial metals (copper).

- Agricultural: wheat, corn, and soybeans.

- Livestock: Pork bellies and feeder cattle.
- Energy: crude oil, petroleum products, and natural gas.

## How you can earn money:

Investors may purchase commodities as a hedge for their portfolios amid inflation. You may acquire commodities indirectly through stocks, mutual funds, for their portfolios amid inflation. You may acquire commodities indirectly through stocks, mutual funds, ETFs, and futures contracts.

## How to Buy Different Types of Investments:

There are two main ways for you to purchase the different types of investments you may be interested in buying. Each is straightforward to accomplish, but only one of the two delivers a service that is totally done for you.
The two strategies to purchase the sorts of assets you desire are:

Start an online brokerage account: You may choose to handle your own investments and only create a brokerage account. This allows you to get up and running fast with the opportunity to purchase stock, bonds, mutual funds, and more in a matter of minutes. The only negative is that you'll be making the ultimate financial choices solely on your own.

**Engage a financial counselor:** The other approach to acquiring several sorts of assets is to hire a financial advisor. The adviser can not only offer you access to purchase and sell assets, but they can also help you work out an overall financial plan and prepare you appropriately for retirement.
This is more of an automated approach in which you only have to authorize transactions or investments, and the adviser takes care of the technicalities.

## Bottom Line

-
There are a number of different sorts of investments to pick from. Some are excellent

for novices, while others demand more skill and investigation.

Each sort of investment provides a distinct amount of risk and return, providing you with a decent alternative or two no matter what your aim may be.

Investors should analyze each form of investment before choosing an asset allocation that matches their overall financial objectives.

## Investing Tips

It might sometimes help to have an expert in your corner while investing. Finding a skilled financial adviser doesn't have to be complicated. SmartAsset's free service connects you with up to three financial advisers that serve your region, and you may interview your advisor matches at no cost to determine which one is ideal for you. If you're ready to locate an adviser who can help you reach your financial objectives, get started today.

If your investments pay off, you may owe capital gains tax. Figure out how much you'll pay when you sell your stocks using our capital gains tax calculator.

# Chapter 5

## 9 SAFE INVESTMENTS WITH THE HIGHEST RETURNS

A large return is what every investor is wanting, but it's not the only element that counts. When analyzing assets, specialists look not just at absolute return possibilities but also something termed "risk-adjusted return."
The basic line is that not all returns are created equal, and wise investors seek to invest where they're receiving the greatest value for the risk that they are taking on—even if that means accepting lower returns.

From that viewpoint, you may favor an investment that pays only 2% a year over one that's yielding 20%. Why? Because if the 2%

return is assured, such as through the U.S. Treasury, but the road to the 20% return carries the chance of losing 40%, that stable 2% might be a superior value over time, based on its low risks—particularly for a risk-averse investor.

For the individual investor, this balance is all the more critical. If you understand how comparing investments entails looking at both returns and risk with equal weight, you may see how even a modest return can be a wonderful bargain if the investment is actually risk-free.

**Here are the nine (9) top safe investments with big returns:**

1. High-yield savings accounts

2. Certificates of deposit

3. Money market accounts

4. Treasury bonds

5. Treasury Inflation-Protected Securities

6. Municipal bonds

7. Corporate bonds

8. S&P 500 index fund or ETF

9. Dividend stocks

You're unlikely to achieve exponential growth with them, but you're even less likely to lose the money you're counting on to keep you and your family safe.

### 1. High-yield savings accounts

The high-yield savings account is pretty much the gold standard of safe investments, delivering excellent returns given the utter lack of danger. The money you have stowed in practically any bank is protected by the Federal Deposit Insurance Corp., meaning the government will make you whole on any losses up to $250,000.

One of the few drawbacks of high-yield savings accounts is that rates might alter in reaction to current market circumstances. When rates are declining, rewards might not appear as appealing.

Rates have been creeping up since early this year, and top high-yield savings accounts are earning above 3% for the first time in a few years. With the national average savings rate hanging at 0.21% as of October 17, high-yield savings accounts are a wonderful value.

Although maybe not as thrilling as prospective stock market gains, high-yield savings accounts are relatively liquid assets, meaning it's simple to access your money without penalty if you need it immediately. That makes stashing your emergency savings something you'd best have if you're genuinely aiming to reduce your financial riskmea really reasonable investment.

Bottom Line: FDIC insurance guarantees your money is 100% secure. It's easy to get a hold of in a hurry, and rates are substantially above the national average savings account rate.

Best for: storing emergency funds; investors looking for risk-free investments.

## 2. Certificates of Deposit

Certificates of deposit are nearly equivalent to savings accounts. Most are FDIC insured, so there's zero danger involved. However, they are still liquid.

With a CD, you accept a time horizon when you invest—generally anything from one month to up to 10 years. Although a few CDs enable you to take the money early without consequence, you normally must pay a penalty if you access your cash before the CD term finishes. On the one hand, it makes CDs far less beneficial for your emergency fund or savings.

On the other hand, it should imply you'll be paid a greater rate of return in exchange for that lack of quick access. Basically, banks will have an easier time reinvesting your funds if you've pledged to leave them alone for a specified length of time. In return, you should obtain a better rate.

**Before you acquire a CD, consider the following:**

Whether or not you could require that money before the CD's maturity date If the answer is yes, you'll want to look elsewhere.

Whether you really are getting a better interest rate than is available with high-yield savings accounts Your only advantage with a CD over a savings account is getting better returns, so if you can find a savings account that pays better than the CDs at your bank, there's just no point.

That said, an FDIC-insured CD's returns might seem modest, but they're pretty stellar in the context of the near-total absence of any risk to you of losing money.

Bottom Line: CDs should offer higher returns than most savings accounts, but that comes at a loss of flexibility, as you'll typically owe a penalty for pulling your money out early.

Best For: Money you can be sure you won't need for the prescribed time frame; investors with a stable financial picture looking to avoid any risk in their investments.

### 3. Money Market Accounts

Money market accounts operate on similar principles to CDs or savings accounts. They usually offer better rates than savings accounts, but they also come with more liquidity and might even let you write checks or use a debit card with the account, allowing for greater flexibility when used alongside a savings account.

If you're using the account just to make deposits and write a monthly rent check, for instance, the MMA could be ideal. However, it has everything to do with the return, so shop around and compare your options not just with other money market accounts but with CDs and high-yield savings accounts as well.

Also, note that the main caveat with a money market account is that many banks will enforce a limit of six transactions a month. If you go over, you'll be fined; if you keep going over, the bank will have to convert your account to a checking account or even close it.

Bottom Line: Money market accounts are very similar to savings accounts but offer the option to write a limited number of checks each month.

***Best For:***

Money that will only be used infrequently; investors who want a little more flexibility than their savings account provides.

***It's good to know***

The FDIC insurance limit of $250,000 is applied per bank and per person, not for each account. So, if you have a savings account, CD, and MMA at the same bank and they have a combined $300,000 in them, you’re not insured on $50,000 of that money.

### 4. Treasury Bonds

Even though a 3% return on a high-yield savings account is more than you're likely to earn on a typical savings account at your bank, you will probably need at least some assets that are taking a little more risk if you want to establish a robust portfolio.

The next rung up from banking products in terms of greater risk and better rewards are bonds, which are effectively structured loans issued to a major corporation.

Treasury bonds, often known as "T-bonds," are backed by the full confidence and credit of the U.S. government. On your end, treasuries will operate much like a CD in many respects. Here's how it works:

You invest with a fixed interest rate and a maturity date ranging from one month to 30 years from the date you purchase the bond.

You'll receive monthly "coupon" payments for the interest while you keep the bond, and then your principal is refunded when the bond expires.

While your coupon payments are absolutely predictable and safe, the face value of your bonds will grow and decrease over time, depending on the prevailing interest rates, stock market performance, and any number of other variables.

Granted, things may turn out in your favor, but only because you've taken on greater risk. So if you aren't pretty convinced you can hold the bond to maturity, it's obviously a riskier investment.

***Keep in mind***

Unlike a CD, you can't draw out your money before the maturity date, not even for a penalty. That doesn't mean you're trapped—you can simply go out and sell the bond on the secondary market. But at that moment, you've gone from purchasing and keeping Treasury bills until maturity, which tends to be highly secure, to trading bonds, which are substantially less safe.

***Bottom Line:***

Debt issued by the Treasury is guaranteed by the full confidence and credit of the U.S. government, making it equally free from danger as FDIC-insured bank accounts.

***Best For:***

Money you know you won't need prior to the maturity date of the bond; money in excess of the $250,000 guaranteed by the FDIC; investors ready to give up some flexibility in quest of somewhat greater returns.

## 5. Treasury Inflation-Protected Securities

Many consumers flock to Treasury Inflation-Protected Securities, or TIPS, in reaction to inflation. Your interest payments will most likely be much lower than what you would earn on a typical Treasury bond during the same time period.

However, you're accepting that lower rate since your principal will rise or fall in value to reflect inflation as assessed by the Consumer Price Index. With inflation hitting 7.7% in October

2022, TIPS investors are doing well while consumers who purchased bonds at a fixed 2% rate are effectively losing 5.7% a year.

Like any other treasury, you expose yourself to all kinds of extra risk if you have to sell TIPS before they mature, so you should be sure you won't need to access that money prior to maturity.

Bottom Line: TIPS give lower yields, but the principal will rise or fall in value depending on the prevailing inflation rates while you keep the bond.

***Best For:***
Money you know you won't need before the bond matures; funds in excess of the $250,000 FDIC insurance limit; investors looking for treasuries but interested in reducing inflation-based risk in their portfolio.

### 6. Municipal Bonds

Municipal bonds, which are issued by state and municipal governments, are a solid alternative for somewhat greater yields with just slightly more risk.

There's basically no danger of the U.S. government failing, but there are undoubtedly incidents of significant cities declaring bankruptcy and losing their bondholders a lot of money.

But most people are undoubtedly aware that a bankruptcy by a big city is very unlikely; however, if you want to be extra cautious, you should stay clear of any cities or states with huge, unmet pension commitments.

And since the federal government has a strong interest in keeping borrowing costs low for state and local governments, it has made income received on munis tax-exempt at the federal level.

In certain circumstances, munis are free from state and local taxes as well. So not only are they typically still secure, but they come with the extra perk of minimizing your tax burden when compared with many other solutions.

Bottom Line: These bonds issued by state and municipal governments are a bit riskier than Treasury bills but come with the plus of being untaxed at the federal level.

Best For: Taking on a little more risk in search of slightly higher profits; investing while keeping your tax burden as low as possible; investors looking for generally secure bonds.

## 7. Corporate Bonds

Like governments of all sizes, companies will likewise issue debt by issuing bonds. Like munis, this might imply you're still in the safe zone, but it's also no sure guarantee.
Plenty of firms that are teetering on the brink of solvency will provide high returns for the high risk—commonly referred to as "junk bonds"—and they aren't a smart pick if you're searching for something genuinely safe.

Although corporate bonds are intrinsically riskier than Treasury bills and frequently riskier than municipal bonds, if you're sticking to huge, blue-chip public corporations and holding the bonds to maturity, they're still in the region of being quite secure.

Fortunately, you're not left to assume how financially stable a firm is. Public corporations typically produce financial reports describing assets, liabilities, and revenue, so you can get a clear picture of where they stand.

And if you, like most people, don't really know your way around a balance sheet or income statement, you may depend on rating organizations like Moody's or S&P Global Ratings. In most circumstances, a AAA-rated bond implies negligible risks if you hold it to maturity.

Bottom Line: These bonds issued by companies are just a little riskier than munis but normally yield just a bit greater interest income.

Best For: A calibrated increase in your portfolio's risk to boost results; investors wishing to diversify their bond holdings

## 8. S&P 500 Index Fund/ETF

Stock markets may be very unpredictable, and on any one day you can win or lose a substantial amount of your investment.

And considering that a GOBankingRates poll of non-investors revealed that the biggest barrier deterring more individuals from purchasing stocks is a lack of cash to commit, it's hard for many families to put at risk money they just freed up for saving by making substantial sacrifices elsewhere.

If you have money you can afford to risk in the stock market, an S&P 500 index mutual fund or exchange-traded fund might be a lower-risk method to get your feet wet.

These funds follow the S&P 500 index, which contains the 500 biggest U.S. public firms as determined by market capitalization. The firms cover a range of market sectors, therefore the S&P 500 is often seen as a gauge of the U.S. stock market and the U.S. economy as a whole.

## Portfolio Diversification

Using index funds or ETFs helps bring diversity to your portfolio. Any one firm may experience a tragedy, but if you purchase shares of a fund that holds stock in numerous companies, you're spreading that risk out by a lot.
All the better if you're purchasing shares in huge, reliable corporations that are regarded as "blue-chip stocks" in investing lingo.

One firm could collapse owing to a crisis, but a few hundred at the same time? It's quite improbable.

## Owning Stocks for the Long Term

Another way to offset most of the risk of stock investing is to hold equities for a very, very long period. While financial markets are highly chaotic over any one week, month, or even year aas proven by an 18.12% decrease in the S&P 500 since the beginning of the year—they actually become very predictable when you look at them in terms of decades.

Over its history, the S&P 500 has returned around 10% a year. And while there have been years when equities dropped 30% or even 40%, the markets have always risen during the following years.

### *It's good to know*

If you had bought an S&P 500 ETF during the 2008 financial crisis, your investment would have lost roughly half its value in only a few months, but over the following eight years, your investment would have averaged 18% each year.

So if you're approaching stock investments as illiquid and only investing money you're certain you won't need to dip into for a few years, you'll have the freedom to wait out a bad downturn in the economy and recover.

## Why choose the S&P 500 index?

The S&P 500 is one of the most popular alternatives for index investing. The index contains practically all blue-chip companies and has a lengthy history of delivering approximately 10% a year—an astounding return considering how little risk is involved over a long time frame.

You may also choose the Russell 1000, which is made up of the 1,000 most valuable American corporations, providing you with twice the diversity.

Bottom Line: Companies are riskier than bonds, but by acquiring huge funds that represent hundreds of stocks and keeping them for extremely long time periods, you may minimize most of the risk and earn significant returns compared with bonds.

Best For: Long-term investments you won't be cashing in for years or even decades; younger investors with lots of time to be patient with the shifting markets; investors interested in increasing their money at a quicker pace than bonds and banking products can supply.

## 9. Dividend Stocks

Dividend stocks offer some exceptionally good possibilities for a few reasons. A dividend is a regular cash payment provided to shareholders—essentially the most direct method a stock may use to send corporate success back to its owners. It also generally signifies several crucial factors for the risk profile of the stock.

**Here are some elements to consider when considering a stock's risk:**

That dividend is far more constant and is paid out whether the stock is up or down. Even if your stock is underperforming in terms of its share value, you're still receiving something back, making it simpler to stay on the stock and wait out a downswing.

The dividend acts as something of a bulwark against falling share prices. Dividends are established as a per-share payment, but investors often concentrate on the "dividend yield," which is the proportion of a company's share price that will be distributed as dividends in a given year. As stock prices decline, you're paying less for that same dividend.

The higher that yield climbs, the tougher it's going to be for bargain-hunting dividend investors to pass it up. That's not going to signify much for a firm that's definitely heading for bankruptcy a lousy investment regardless of the dividend yield but it will help prop up the share price for a company that's merely going through some difficult times.

Companies may and will decrease their payouts in times of great hardship. It's rare, as it usually results in the stock plunging. Consistency is what people like about dividends, so they tend to react very poorly when a dividend appears less secure.
But dividend payments are less secure than the coupon payment on a bond, for example, which is fixed.

That said, if you look around for firms that not only give a significant yield but have a lengthy track record of regularly growing their dividend on a regular basis — often referred to as "dividend aristocrats" — you may reduce a lot of that risk.

Bottom Line: Owning stock in an individual firm is significantly riskier than the other alternatives, but dividend stocks will give a regular return whether markets are up or down.

Best for: Long-term investments that still generate passive income; investors seeking to create a regular income stream; and younger investors reinvesting dividends to maximize growth.

## How do safe investments with high returns stack up?

The ideal portfolio is one with both minimal risk and maximum returns. There's always some sacrifice required to reach the correct balance. Although the relative predictability provided by your savings account is fantastic, the earnings it will generate aren't nearly enough on their own to genuinely create wealth.

Likewise, although the returns delivered by an S&P 500 fund are significantly greater over the long run, it's crucial to look at them from the perspective of the risk that you must take—

mmost notably, the danger of double-digit percentage losses over the short term—that insured banking products simply don’t have.

**Here are some of the questions people ask when deciding where to invest their money.**

- What is the safest investment with the highest return?

- Unfortunately, the safest investments don't provide the highest returns. However, a savings account is the safest place to keep your money, and a high-yield account can provide decent returns.

- Which investments give the highest returns?

- Stocks provide the highest average annual returns: 13.8% on average, compared to 1.6% on bonds, 0.8% on gold, 8.8% on real estate, and 0.38% on CDs, according to Fidelity.

- What are the three safest investment types?

- The three safest investments are savings accounts, CDs, and Treasury bonds.

www.ingramcontent.com/pod-product-compliance
Lightning Source LLC
LaVergne TN
LVHW020524160826
845677LV00015B/3889

*9798367624670*